# Home for the Holidays

## QUILTS & MORE TO WELCOME THE SEASON

**Sherri McConnell & Chelsi Stratton**

C&T PUBLISHING
*Another Maker Inspired!*

Publisher: Amy Barrett-Daffin
Creative Director: Gailen Runge
Senior Editor: Roxane Cerda
Technical Editor: Nancy Mahoney
Copy Editor: Melissa Bryan
Illustrator: Sandy Loi
Book Designer: Adrienne Smitke
Photographers: Adam Albright and Brent Kane
Production Coordinator: Zinnia Heinzmann

Published by C&T Publishing, Inc., P.O. Box 1456, Lafayette, CA 94549

Library of Congress Control Number: 2023935135

Printed in the USA

10 9 8 7 6 5 4 3 2

**SPECIAL THANKS**

*Photography for this book was taken at the home of Jodi Allen in Woodinville, Washington.*

# Contents

# Introduction

We first started talking about ideas for this mother-daughter book several years ago on a flight home from International Quilt Market. Sherri remembers pulling out her phone and putting in a few notes about the idea. Every now and again we revisited the topic, and it's exciting to see it finally come to fruition. Why a Christmas book, you might ask? One reason we both love Christmas may be primarily because of the influence of Sherri's grandmother, who absolutely loved the holidays and the chance to gather her family around her. She and Sherri's grandfather left a lovely retirement community and lifestyle in Florida to move closer to grandchildren when their age prevented them from traveling in their motorhome. As the great-grandchildren arrived, Grandma took great delight in having them over for game nights and holiday preparations. And each Christmas, every member of the family received at least one "soft" package with something handmade by Grandma. It might have been a set of pot holders, place mats, or a pillow. But there was something handmade each year for every family member—gifts that she had worked on throughout the year.

While we both love Christmas decorating and especially Christmas quilts, we do have decidedly different styles. Sherri's designs and projects tend toward the classic and simple, while Chelsi has a modern flair and a knack for incorporating unique contemporary items into her decor. With many of the projects in this book we split the available fabrics, so it's been fun to see the different takes inspired by the same collection of prints. We shared some initial concept ideas but then didn't share again until we had completed projects, so there was also a nice element of surprise in this compilation.

We hope that you'll enjoy creating your own Christmas quilts and decor items with this variety of patterns, and we also hope that you'll find the tips and ideas scattered throughout the book to be useful as you create your own traditions or help your family and friends enjoy their personal traditions with a quilted Christmas.

~ Sherri and Chelsi

# Christmas Eve Lap Quilt

*One of my favorite star patterns is the traditional Sawtooth Star with a square-in-a-square unit for the center. This design offers many opportunities to play with a scrappy mix of fabrics, even when using fabrics from one collection. The fabric collection I chose contained a lovely mix of reds, greens, grays, and low-volume prints, which were perfect to mix and match in these Star blocks. Although this design is beautiful using a coordinated fabric collection, it would also make a wonderful scrap quilt using leftover pieces from a variety of Christmas projects. Additionally, since I had lots of leftover triangles from this project, I sewed them together and used the resulting half-square-triangle units for two more projects. ~ Sherri*

**FINISHED QUILT: 62½" × 62½"**
**FINISHED BLOCK: 12" × 12"**

## MATERIALS

*Yardage is based on 42"-wide fabric. Fat quarters measure 18" × 21"; fat eighths measure 9" × 21". Fabrics are from the Christmas Morning fabric group by Vanessa Goertzen of Lella Boutique for Moda Fabrics.*

* 16 fat quarters of assorted red, green, and gray prints (referred to collectively as "dark") for blocks
* 2¼ yards of white solid for blocks and inner border
* 6 fat eighths of light gray prints (referred to collectively as "light") for blocks
* ½ yard of gray solid for sashing
* 1 fat eighth of green check for cornerstones
* ⅞ yard of red floral for outer border
* ½ yard of red dot for binding
* 3⅞ yards of fabric for backing
* 69" × 69" piece of batting

## CUTTING

*All measurements include ¼"-wide seam allowances.*

**From *each* of the dark prints, cut:**
12 squares, 3½" × 3½" (192 total)

**From the white solid, cut:**
17 strips, 3½" × 42"; crosscut into:
    64 pieces, 3½" × 6½"
    64 squares, 3½" × 3½"
6 strips, 1¾" × 42"

**From *each* of the light prints, cut:**
3 squares, 6½" × 6½" (18 total; 2 are extra)

**From the gray solid, cut:**
8 strips, 2" × 42"; crosscut into 24 strips, 2" × 12½"

**From the green check, cut:**
9 squares, 2" × 2"

**From the red floral, cut:**
6 strips, 4" × 42"

**From the red dot, cut:**
7 strips, 2¼" × 42"

## MAKING THE BLOCKS

Press seam allowances in the directions indicated by the arrows.

**1.** Draw a diagonal line from corner to corner on the wrong side of the dark 3½" squares. Place a marked square on one end of a white 3½" × 6½" piece, right sides together. Sew on the marked line. Trim the excess corner fabric ¼" from the stitched line. Place a marked square on the opposite end of the white piece. Sew and trim as before to make a flying-geese unit measuring 3½" × 6½", including seam allowances. Make 16 sets of four matching units. If desired, save the trimmed triangles to make half-square-triangle units (see "Bonus Units" at right).

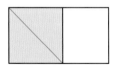 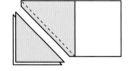

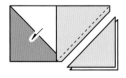 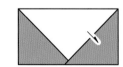

Make 16 sets of 4 matching units, 3½" × 6½".

**2.** Using the remaining marked squares from step 1, place matching squares on opposite corners of a light 6½" square. Sew on the marked lines. Trim

the excess corner fabric ¼" from the stitched lines. Place matching marked squares on the remaining corners of the square. Sew and trim as before to make a center unit. Make 16 units measuring 6½" square, including seam allowances. If desired, save the trimmed triangles to make half-square-triangle units (refer again to "Bonus Units").

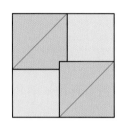 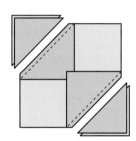

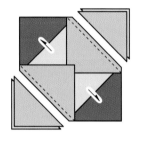 

Make 16 units, 6½" × 6½".

**3.** Lay out four white 3½" squares, four matching flying-geese units, and one contrasting center unit in three rows. Sew the pieces into rows, and then join the rows to make a Star block. Make 16 blocks measuring 12½" square, including seam allowances.

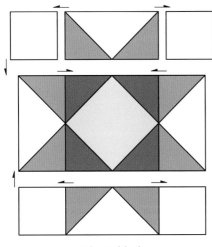

Make 16 blocks,
12½" × 12½".

## ASSEMBLING THE QUILT TOP

Refer to the photo on page 10 for color placement as needed.

**1.** Join four blocks and three gray solid strips to make a block row. Make four rows measuring 12½" × 53", including seam allowances.

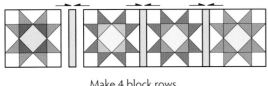

Make 4 block rows,
12½" × 53".

**2.** Join four gray solid strips and three green check squares to make a sashing row. Make three rows measuring 2" × 53", including seam allowances.

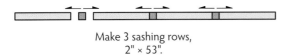

Make 3 sashing rows,
2" × 53".

## A Note from Chelsi

*Mom's Christmas Eve Lap Quilt is so fun and vibrant! My great-grandma often made smaller quilts that were always readily available to use when we visited, and I have noticed that my mom makes similar-sized projects as well. This lap quilt is a sweet reminder to me of my great-grandma and is the perfect project to make if you prefer something smaller in size.*

*Designed and pieced by Sherri McConnell; quilted by Marion Bott*

**3.** Join the block rows and sashing rows, alternating their positions as shown in the quilt assembly diagram below. The quilt top should measure 53" square, including seam allowances.

**4.** Join the white 1¾"-wide strips end to end. From the pieced strip, cut two 55½"-long strips and two 53"-long strips. Sew the shorter strips to the left and right sides of the quilt center. Sew the longer strips to the top and bottom edges. The quilt top should measure 55½" square, including seam allowances.

**5.** Join the red floral strips end to end. From the pieced strip, cut two 62½"-long strips and two 55½"-long strips. Sew the shorter strips to the left and right sides of the quilt center. Sew the longer strips to the top and bottom edges. The quilt top should measure 62½" square.

## FINISHING THE QUILT

**1.** Layer the quilt top with batting and backing; baste the layers together.

**2.** Quilt by hand or machine. The quilt shown is machine quilted with an allover diamond and pumpkin-seed design.

**3.** Use the red dot 2¼"-wide strips to make double-fold binding and then attach the binding to the quilt.

Quilt assembly

# Waiting for Santa

When I made the Christmas Eve Lap Quilt (page 7) I ended up with a lot of very usable scraps that could easily be turned into half-square triangles. Why not use them (or any of your scraps) to make a coordinating pillow sham? It uses a standard bed pillow as the insert, and looks equally great on a sofa or as a decorative accent on a bed. While you're at it, use some of those triangles to treat yourself—or Santa—to a fun mug rug! ~ Sherri

## Waiting for Santa Pillow

### FINISHED PILLOW: 26½" × 20½"

## MATERIALS

*Yardage is based on 42"-wide fabric. If you are using bonus triangle units from the Christmas Eve Lap Quilt (page 7), you do not need the assorted dark and light 3" squares.*

* 65 squares, 3" × 3" *each*, of assorted dark prints in red, green, and gray for patchwork
* 65 squares, 3" × 3" *each*, of assorted light prints for patchwork
* ⅞ yard of fabric for pillow back
* ⅛ yard of coordinating print for zipper flap
* ¼ yard of red dot for binding
* 1⅝ yards of muslin for quilt-sandwich backing
* 25" × 31" piece of batting for pillow front
* 27" × 32" piece of batting for pillow back
* 20" × 26" pillow form
* 28" zipper

### Zipper Tip from Sherri

*I use the zipper tape on a roll from ByAnnie. I can cut the tape to the desired size easily, and then I add zipper tabs as needed.*

## CUTTING

*All measurements include ¼" seam allowances.*

**From the pillow-back fabric, cut:**
1 piece, 27" × 32"

**From the coordinating print, cut:**
1 strip, 4" × 27½"

**From the red dot, cut:**
3 strips, 2¼" × 42"

**From the muslin, cut:**
1 piece, 25" × 31"
1 piece, 27" × 32"

### A Note from Chelsi

*Mom always has fun pillows on almost every bed or couch in her home. They are the perfect way to spruce up any space, and they're good to have around because they're so cozy. This pillow design uses half-square triangles that draw your eyes in without overpowering any of your other decor.*

## ASSEMBLING THE PILLOW TOP

If you're using bonus triangle units from the Christmas Eve Lap Quilt, skip step 1 and trim 130 units to 2½" square. Press seam allowances in the directions indicated by the arrows.

**1.** Draw a diagonal line from corner to corner on the wrong side of the light 3" squares. Layer a marked square on a dark 3" square, right sides together. Sew ¼" from both sides of the drawn line. Cut the unit apart on the marked line to make two half-square-triangle units. Trim the units to measure 2½" square, including seam allowances. Make 130 units.

Make 130 units.

**2.** Lay out the half-square-triangle units in 10 rows of 13 units each, as shown. Sew the units into rows and then join the rows. The pillow top should measure 26½" × 20½".

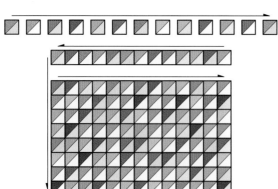

Make 1 pillow top, 26½" × 20½".

**3.** Layer the pillow top with the 25" × 31" pieces of batting and muslin; baste the layers together. Quilt by hand or machine. The pillow top shown is machine quilted with an allover leaf and swirl design.

## MAKING THE PILLOW BACK

Refer to "Making the Pillow Back" on page 27 of the Christmas Star Pillow project for detailed illustrations.

**1.** Layer the pillow-back piece with the 27" × 32" pieces of batting and muslin; baste the layers together. Quilt by hand or machine.

**2.** Cut the quilted pillow back into two 11½" × 27½" pieces.

**3.** Press the print 4" × 27½" strip in half, wrong sides together, so that it measures 2" × 27½". This will be the zipper flap.

**4.** Align the flap right sides together with the raw edge of a quilted pillow-back piece. Place the zipper along the raw edges, right sides together. The zipper edge should be aligned with the raw edges of the flap and pillow back. Any extra zipper length should extend beyond the fabric. It will be trimmed later. Use a zipper foot to sew the zipper using a ¼" seam allowance.

**5.** Place the second quilted pillow-back piece right sides together with the unsewn side of the zipper, aligning the zipper edge with the raw edge of the pillow back. Pin and sew the zipper in place using a ¼" seam allowance and a zipper foot.

*Designed and pieced by Sherri McConnell; quilted by Vicky Willard*

**6.** Press the seam with the flap so that it covers the zipper; topstitch ¼" from the flap seam.

## Table Topper

*Take out the pillow form and you can use the pillow sham as a charming table topper. It would look particularly beautiful displayed in the same room where you're using a quilt made with identical fabrics.*

## FINISHING THE PILLOW

**1.** Place the pillow front on the pillow back, wrong sides together. Unzip the zipper partway so that the zipper pull is in the center of the pillow. Pin and sew around the edges using a ¼" seam allowance. Trim any excess length from the end of the zipper. Trim the pillow back even with the pillow top.

**2.** Use the red dot 2¼"-wide strips to make double-fold binding and then bind the pillow as you would a quilt.

**3.** Unzip the pillow. Insert the pillow form and close the zipper.

# Waiting for Santa Mug Rug

**FINISHED MUG RUG: 10½" × 8½"**

## MATERIALS

*Yields 1 mug rug. Yardage is based on 42"-wide fabric. Fat quarters measure 18" × 21"; fat eighths measure 9" × 21". If you are using bonus triangle units from the Christmas Eve Lap Quilt (page 7), you do not need the assorted dark and light 3" squares.*

* 6 squares, 3" × 3" *each*, of assorted dark prints in red, green, and gray for patchwork
* 6 squares, 3" × 3" *each*, of assorted light prints for patchwork
* 1 fat eighth of cream stripe for border
* 1 fat eighth of red dot for binding
* 1 fat quarter of fabric for backing
* 13" × 15" piece of batting

### Make It Your Own

*Each mug rug uses just 12 half-square triangles. If you're not using leftover triangle units from the Christmas Eve Lap Quilt, feel free to use a scrappy mix of triangles, or make them all the same. Either combination creates a fun mug rug.*

## CUTTING

*All measurements include ¼" seam allowances.*

**From the cream stripe, cut:**
2 strips, 1½" × 10½"
2 strips, 1½" × 6½"

**From the red dot, cut:**
3 strips, 2¼" × 21"

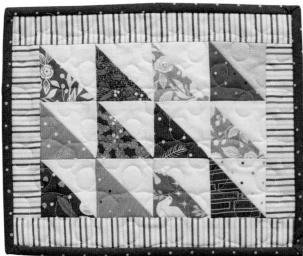

*Designed and pieced by Sherri McConnell; quilted by Vicky Willard*

## A Note from Chelsi

*I love that Mom added these mug rugs to her list of projects! You can make these up quickly for each member of your household (plus a few more for guests). They're the perfect addition to any chilly night when you need a good steaming cup of hot chocolate. Oh, and don't forget the marshmallows!*

## ASSEMBLING THE MUG RUG

If you're using bonus triangle units from the Christmas Eve Lap Quilt, skip step 1 and trim 12 units to 2½" square. Press seam allowances in the directions indicated by the arrows.

**1.** Draw a diagonal line from corner to corner on the wrong side of the light 3" squares. Layer a marked square on a dark 3" square, right sides together. Sew ¼" from both sides of the drawn line. Cut the unit apart on the marked line to make two half-square-triangle units. Trim the units to measure 2½" square, including seam allowances. Make 12 units.

Make 12 units.

**2.** Lay out the half-square-triangle units in three rows of four units each, with all the units oriented in the same direction. Sew the units into rows and then join the rows. The mug rug should measure 8½" × 6½", including seam allowances.

**3.** Sew the cream stripe 1½" × 6½" strips to the left and right sides of the mug-rug center. Sew the cream stripe 1½" × 10½" strips to the top and bottom edges. The mug rug should measure 10½" × 8½".

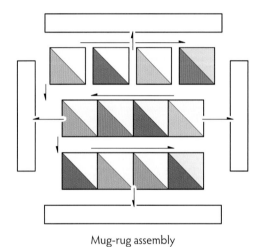

Mug-rug assembly

## FINISHING THE MUG RUG

**1.** Layer the mug-rug top with batting and backing; baste the layers together.

**2.** Quilt by hand or machine. The mug rug shown is machine quilted with an allover loop design.

**3.** Use the red dot 2¼"-wide strips to make double-fold binding and then attach the binding to the mug rug.

# Peppermint Twist

*My great-grandmother had a crystal bowl that she filled with assorted candies for anyone to eat during the holidays. I always chose the peppermints that were mixed up in the bowl. Unsurprisingly, the candies were often eaten up very quickly. But without fail, the bowl was always refilled every time my family visited. These days I always crave a peppermint candy during the Christmas season. ~ Chelsi*

**FINISHED QUILT: 58½" × 67½"**
**FINISHED BLOCK: 9" × 9"**

## MATERIALS

*Yardage is based on 42"-wide fabric. Fabrics are from various collections by Sherri & Chelsi for Moda Fabrics.*

* 3 yards of white solid for block backgrounds and border
* ⅜ yard *each* of 3 assorted red prints for blocks
* ½ yard *each* of 3 assorted green prints for blocks and binding
* 3⅝ yards of fabric for backing
* 65" × 74" piece of batting

## CUTTING

*All measurements include ¼" seam allowances.*

**From the white solid, cut:**
3 strips, 4" × 42"; crosscut into 21 squares, 4" × 4"
19 strips, 3½" × 42"; crosscut into:
    42 pieces, 3½" × 6½"
    126 squares, 3½" × 3½"
7 strips, 2½" × 42"

**From *each* of the assorted red prints, cut:**
3 strips, 3½" × 42"; crosscut into:
    7 strips, 3½" × 9½" (21 total)
    14 squares, 3½" × 3½" (42 total)

**From *each* of the assorted green prints, cut:**
1 strip, 4" × 42"; crosscut into 7 squares, 4" × 4" (21 total)
1 strip, 3½" × 42"; crosscut into 7 squares, 3½" × 3½" (21 total)
3 strips, 2¼" × 42"; crosscut into 8 strips, 2¼" × 11" (24 total)

### Organization Saves Time

*After cutting your fabrics, separate everything by matching print and color. This will help keep you organized and on task when piecing your blocks.*

## MAKING THE CROSS BLOCKS

Press seam allowances in the directions indicated by the arrows.

**1.** Join two white 3½" squares and one red 3½" square to make an A unit measuring 3½" × 9½", including seam allowances. Repeat to make 21 pairs of matching A units (42 total).

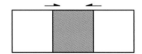

Make 21 pairs of matching A units,
3½" × 9½".

**2.** Sew matching A units to the top and bottom of a matching red 3½" × 9½" strip to make a block. Make 21 Cross blocks measuring 9½" square, including seam allowances.

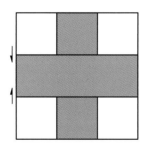

Make 21 Cross blocks,
9½" × 9½".

## MAKING THE TWIST BLOCKS

**1.** Draw a diagonal line from corner to corner on the wrong side of the white 4" squares. Layer a marked square on a green 4" square, right sides together. Sew ¼" from both sides of the drawn line. Cut the unit apart on the marked line to make two half-square-triangle units. Trim the units to measure 3½" square, including seam allowances. Make 42 units.

Make 42 units.

**2.** Sew a triangle unit from step 1 to one end of a white 3½" × 6½" piece to make a B unit measuring 3½" × 9½", including seam allowances. Make 21 pairs of matching B units (42 total).

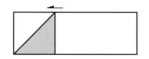

Make 21 pairs of matching B units,
3½" × 9½".

**3.** Sew white 3½" squares to opposite sides of a green 3½" square to make a C unit measuring 3½" × 9½", including seam allowances. Make 21 C units.

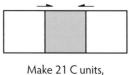

Make 21 C units,
3½" × 9½".

*Designed and pieced by Chelsi Stratton; quilted by Marion Bott*

**4.** Using matching green prints, sew B units to the top and bottom of a C unit to make a block. Make 21 Twist blocks measuring 9½" square, including seam allowances.

## ASSEMBLING THE QUILT TOP

**1.** Referring to the quilt assembly diagram on page 22, arrange the blocks in seven rows of six blocks each, starting with the Cross block and alternating the blocks in each row and from row to row. Sew the blocks into rows and

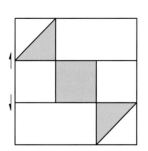

Make 21 Twist blocks,
9½" × 9½".

then join the rows. The quilt top should measure 54½" × 63½", including seam allowances.

**2.** Join the white 2½"-wide strips end to end. From the pieced strip, cut two 63½"-long strips and two 58½"-long strips. Sew the longer strips to the left and right sides of the quilt center. Sew the shorter strips to the top and bottom edges. The quilt top should measure 58½" × 67½".

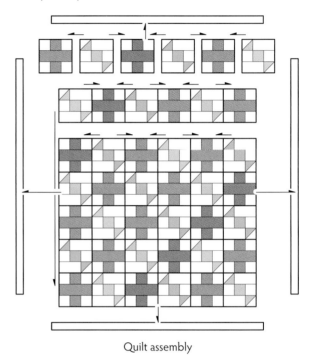

Quilt assembly

## FINISHING THE QUILT

**1.** Layer the quilt top with batting and backing; baste the layers together.

**2.** Quilt by hand or machine. The quilt shown is machine quilted with an allover design of circles and flowers.

**3.** Use the green 2¼"-wide strips to make scrappy double-fold binding and then attach the binding to the quilt.

# Christmas Star Pillow

*When my husband and I were first married, we started the tradition of going out to cut down our very own Christmas tree every year. It became an annual adventure filled with memories that I'm ever so fond of. Years later we still enjoy the experience, and our children love it as well. This fun pillow reminds me of that special tradition we created, and I think it will look adorable in any home. ~ Chelsi*

**FINISHED PILLOW: 18½" × 18½"**

## MATERIALS

*Yardage is based on 42"-wide fabric. Fabrics are Hustle & Bustle by Basic Grey for Moda Fabrics.*

* ¼ yard *total* of assorted green prints for tree
* ⅜ yard of white solid for background
* ⅛ yard of gray print for tree trunk and star
* ⅓ yard of light print for pillow back
* ⅓ yard of red print for zipper flap and binding
* 22" × 22" square of muslin for quilt-sandwich backing
* 22" × 22" square of batting
* 18" × 18" pillow form
* 20" zipper

## CUTTING

*All measurements include ¼" seam allowances.*

From the assorted green prints, cut a *total* of:
1 A piece, 2½" × 4½"
1 B piece, 2½" × 6½"
1 C piece, 2½" × 8½"
1 D piece, 2½" × 10½"
1 E piece, 2½" × 12½"
1 F piece, 2½" × 14½"

From the white solid, cut:
4 strips, 2½" × 42"; crosscut into:
    1 strip, 2½" × 18½"
    1 strip, 2½" × 14½"
    2 pieces, 2½" × 8½"
    1 piece, 2½" × 7½"
    1 piece, 2½" × 6½"
    2 pieces, 2½" × 5½"
    2 pieces, 2½" × 4½"
    3 pieces, 2½" × 3½"
    20 squares, 2½" × 2½"

From the gray print, cut:
2 squares, 2½" × 2½"
8 squares, 1½" × 1½"

From the light print, cut:
1 strip, 9¼" × 42"; crosscut into 2 pieces, 9¼" × 18½"

From the red print, cut:
1 strip, 4" × 18½"
2 strips, 2¼" × 42"

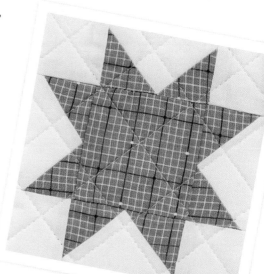

## MAKING THE PILLOW TOP

Press seam allowances in the directions indicated by the arrows.

**1.** Draw a diagonal line from corner to corner on the wrong side of 12 white 2½" squares. Place a marked square on one end of the green A piece, right sides together. Sew on the marked line. Trim the excess corner fabric ¼" from the stitched line. Place a marked square on the opposite end of the green piece. Sew and trim as before to make an A unit measuring 2½" × 4½", including seam allowances.

Make 1 A unit,
2½" × 4½".

**2.** Repeat step 1 using the marked white squares and the green B–F pieces to make the units shown in the diagram.

Make 1 B unit,      Make 1 C unit,
2½" × 6½".         2½" × 8½".

Make 1 D unit,
2½" × 10½".

Make 1 E unit,
2½" × 12½".

Make 1 F unit,
2½" × 14½".

**3.** Draw a diagonal line from corner to corner on the wrong side of the gray 1½" squares. Repeat step 1 using two marked gray squares and one white 2½" square. Make three small star-point units measuring 2½" square, including seam allowances. In the same way, sew marked gray squares to adjacent corners of a white 2½" × 3½" piece to make one large star-point unit.

Make 3 units,     Make 1 unit,
2½" × 2½".       2½" × 3½".

**4.** Referring to the diagram, lay out the A–F units, the gray 2½" squares, the star-point units, and the white pieces in nine rows, placing the large star-point unit on the left side of the gray square in the second row. Sew the pieces into rows. Join the rows to make the pillow top, which should measure 18½" square, including seam allowances.

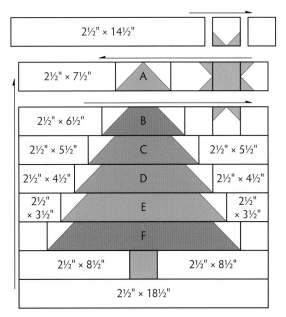

Pillow-top assembly

*Designed and pieced by Chelsi Stratton; quilted by Gail Begay*

**5.** Layer the pillow top, batting, and muslin square; baste the layers together.

**6.** Quilt by hand or machine. The pillow top shown is machine quilted with diagonal crosshatch lines.

**7.** Trim the excess batting and backing even with the pillow top.

## MAKING THE PILLOW BACK

**1.** Press the red 4" × 18½" strip in half, wrong sides together, so that it measures 2" × 18½". This will be the zipper flap.

**2.** Align the flap right sides together with the raw edge of a light 9¼" × 18½" piece. Place the zipper along the raw edges, right sides together. The zipper edge should be aligned with the raw edges of the flap and pillow back. Any extra zipper length should extend beyond the fabric. It will be trimmed later. Use a zipper foot to sew the zipper using a ¼" seam allowance.

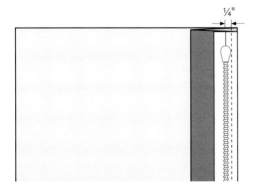

**3.** Fold the flap away. Place the second light 9¼" × 18½" piece right sides together with the unsewn side of the zipper, aligning the zipper edge with the raw edge of the pillow back. Pin and sew the zipper in place using a ¼" seam allowance and a zipper foot.

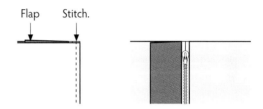

**4.** Press the seam with the flap so that it covers the zipper; topstitch ¼" from the flap seam.

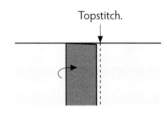

## FINISHING THE PILLOW

**1.** Place the pillow front on the pillow back, wrong sides together. Unzip the zipper partway so that the zipper pull is in the center of the pillow. Pin and sew around the edges using a ¼" seam allowance. Trim any excess length from the end of the zipper.

**2.** Use the red 2¼"-wide strips to make binding and then bind the pillow as you would a quilt.

**3.** Unzip the pillow. Insert the pillow form and close the zipper.

# Crystal Sky Table Mates

*It's always a bit hard to put away the Christmas decor, so recently I've been making more winter-themed projects using various shades of blue. This delightful Ohio Star table runner and coaster set makes the perfect backdrop for a winter gathering. You'll definitely want to use them until the snow thaws! ~ Sherri*

## Crystal Sky Runner

**FINISHED RUNNER: 15½" × 55½"**
**FINISHED BLOCK: 9" × 9"**

## MATERIALS

*Yardage is based on 42"-wide fabric. Fat quarters measure 18" × 21"; fat eighths measure 9" × 21". Fabrics are from the Crystal Lane collection by Anne Sutton of Bunny Hill Designs for Moda Fabrics.*

* 3 fat quarters of assorted medium blue prints (referred to collectively as "blue") for blocks and outer border
* 2 fat eighths of navy prints for blocks
* 1 fat quarter of light blue print for blocks
* 1 fat eighth of blue stripe for blocks
* 2 fat quarters of white dot for blocks*
* ⅓ yard of white solid for sashing and inner border
* ⅓ yard of navy solid for binding
* 1¾ yards of fabric for backing
* 22" × 62" piece of batting

*\*The quilt shown uses 2 slightly different white dot fabrics. If you prefer to use just 1 white dot, you'll need ½ yard.*

29

## CUTTING

*All measurements include ¼" seam allowances.*
*As you cut, keep like prints together.*

**From *each* of the blue and navy prints, cut:**
2 squares, 4½" × 4½" (10 total)
1 square, 3½" × 3½" (5 total)

**From the remainder of the blue prints,
cut a *total* of:**
2 strips, 2½" × 11½"
12 strips, 2½" × 10"

**From the light blue print, cut:**
5 squares, 4½" × 4½"

**From the blue stripe, cut:**
20 squares, 2½" × 2½"

**From *1* white dot, cut:**
3 squares, 4½" × 4½"
12 squares, 3½" × 3½"

**From the remaining white dot, cut:**
2 squares, 4½" × 4½"
8 squares, 3½" × 3½"

**From the white solid, cut:**
5 strips, 1½" × 42"; crosscut *2 of the strips* into
    6 strips, 1½" × 9½"

**From the navy solid, cut:**
4 strips, 2¼" × 42"

## MAKING THE BLOCKS

Directions are for making one block. Repeat to make a total of five blocks. Press seam allowances in the directions indicated by the arrows.

**1.** For each block, choose the following:

**White dot:** one 4½" square and four 3½" squares

**Light blue:** one 4½" square

**Blue or navy:** two 4½" squares and one 3½" square

**Blue stripe:** four 2½" squares

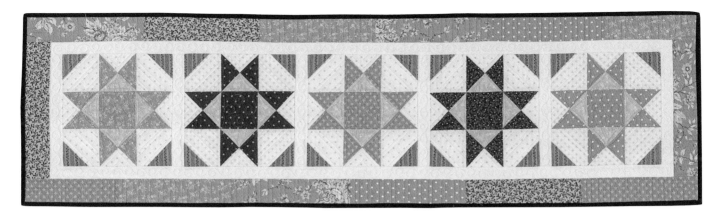

*Designed and pieced by Sherri McConnell; quilted by Val Krueger*

**2.** Draw a diagonal line from corner to corner on the wrong side of a white dot and a light blue 4½" square. Layer the marked white dot square on a blue or navy 4½" square, right sides together. Sew ¼" from both sides of the drawn line. Cut the unit apart on the marked line to make two half-square-triangle units. The units should measure 4⅛" square, including seam allowances. Repeat using the marked light blue square and a blue or navy square to make two half-square-triangle units.

Make 2 of each unit,
4⅛" × 4⅛".

**3.** On the wrong side of each white/blue triangle unit, draw a diagonal line from corner to corner. Placed a marked unit right sides together with a light blue/blue triangle unit. Make sure contrasting fabrics are facing each other and the marked unit is on top. Butt the diagonal seam allowances against each other. Sew ¼" from both sides of the drawn line; cut on the marked line to make two hourglass units. Trim the units to measure 3½" square, including seam allowances. Repeat to make a total of four hourglass units.

Make 4 units.

**4.** Draw a diagonal line from corner to corner on the wrong side of the blue stripe 2½" squares. Place a marked square on the upper-left corner of a white dot 3½" square. Sew along the marked line. Trim the excess corner fabric ¼" from the stitched line. Make two corner units measuring 3½" square, including seam allowances. Repeat to make two mirror-image corner units by placing the marked square on the upper-right corner of the white dot square.

Make 2 of each unit,
3½" × 3½".

**5.** Lay out the four corner units, four hourglass units, and one matching blue 3½" square in three rows. Sew the pieces into rows. Join the rows to make a block measuring 9½" square, including seam allowances. Repeat the steps to make a total of five blocks.

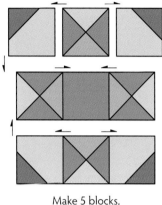

Make 5 blocks,
9½" × 9½".

## ASSEMBLING THE TABLE-RUNNER TOP

**1.** Referring to the table-runner assembly diagram below, lay out the blocks and white solid 1½" × 9½" strips, starting with a white strip and alternating their positions. Join the pieces to make a row measuring 9½" × 51½", including seam allowances.

**2.** Join the remaining white solid 1½"-wide strips end to end. From the pieced strip, cut two 51½"-long strips. Sew the strips to the long edges of the table-runner center. The table-runner top should measure 11½" × 51½", including seam allowances.

**3.** Sew the blue 2½" × 11½" strips to the short ends of the table runner. Join six blue 2½" × 10" strips, alternating the prints, to make a strip. Make two strips. Press the seam allowances in one direction and then trim the strips to 55½" long. Sew these strips to the long edges. The table runner should measure 15½" × 55½".

> ### Plan Ahead
>
> *I always lay out the pieces for the long outer-border strips before sewing them together to make sure I have a nice arrangement and none of the same prints are next to each other. ~ Sherri*

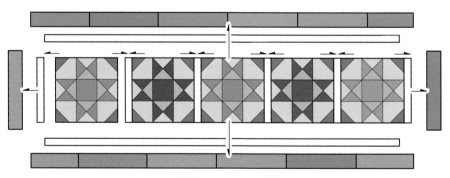

Table-runner assembly

## FINISHING THE TABLE RUNNER

**1.** Layer the table-runner top with batting and backing; baste the layers together.

**2.** Quilt by hand or machine. The table runner shown is machine quilted with straight lines along the seamlines in the blocks and a circular motif in the block centers. Loops are stitched in the inner border and sashing. Evenly spaced lines are stitched in the outer border.

**3.** Use the navy solid 2¼"-wide strips to make double-fold binding and then attach the binding to the table runner.

# Super Sugar Cookies

Our family sugar cookie recipe has been the favorite for more than a quarter of a century. These puffy sugar cookies are terrific for frosting, they don't require refrigeration of the dough before cutting, and they can easily be made a day ahead if needed. I'll often make and bake the cookies and then freeze ahead of time so that the baking and the frosting aren't done on the same day.

2 cups sugar
1 cup butter
3 eggs
1 cup milk
1 teaspoon baking soda
4 teaspoons baking powder
½ teaspoon salt
1 teaspoon vanilla
6 cups (or more) all-purpose flour

Preheat oven to 375°. Mix sugar and butter. Add eggs. Mix the dry ingredients in a separate bowl and add them to the sugar, butter, and eggs, alternating with milk. You can roll out the dough and cut out the desired shapes, or refrigerate to cut out later. Bake 12 minutes.

# Crystal Sky Coaster

**FINISHED COASTER: 5" × 5"**

## MATERIALS

*Yields 1 coaster. Fabrics are from the Crystal Lane collection by Anne Sutton of Bunny Hill Designs for Moda Fabrics.*

* 7" × 7" square of blue print for star
* 6" × 9" square of light print for background
* 1 strip, 2" × 42", of navy solid for binding
* 8" × 8" square of fabric for backing
* 8" × 8" square of batting

---

### Quick Gifts

*A set of quilted coasters makes a practical and cute gift. Tie together a set of four with a Christmas ribbon or roll up a couple and place them in a fun mug for a hostess or coworker gift, or for when a neighbor drops by unexpectedly during the holidays.*

---

## CUTTING

*All measurements include ¼" seam allowances.*

**From the blue print, cut:**
2 squares, 3" × 3"
1 square, 2" × 2"

**From the light print, cut:**
2 squares, 3" × 3"
4 squares, 2" × 2"

## MAKING THE BLOCK

*Press seam allowances in the directions indicated by the arrows.*

**1.** Draw a diagonal line from corner to corner on the wrong side of the light 3" squares. Layer a marked square on a blue 3" square, right sides together. Sew ¼" from both sides of the drawn line. Cut the unit apart on the marked line to make two half-square-triangle units. The units should measure 2⅝" square, including seam allowances. Make a total of four half-square-triangle units.

Make 4 units,
2⅝" × 2⅝".

**A Note from Chelsi**

*I love the Ohio Star blocks in these Crystal Sky Coasters, and I also love the sweet simplicity of this project. I often find myself looking for smaller projects that can be finished quickly, and this one fills the bill perfectly.*

**2.** On the wrong side of two triangle units from step 1, draw a diagonal line from corner to corner. Place a marked unit right sides together with an unmarked triangle unit. Make sure contrasting fabrics are facing each other and the marked unit is on top. Butt the diagonal seam allowances against each other. Sew ¼" from both sides of the drawn line; cut on the marked line to make two hourglass units. Trim the units to measure 2" square, including seam allowances. Repeat to make a total of four hourglass units.

Make 4 units.

**3.** Lay out the four light 2" squares, four hourglass units, and one blue 2" square in three rows. Sew the pieces into rows. Join the rows to make a block measuring 5" square, including seam allowances.

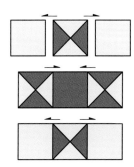 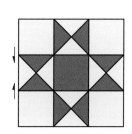

Make 1 block,
5" × 5".

> **Binding Tip from Sherri**
>
> *Binding small quilted items can be a little tricky. I find it's best to start sewing just before the corner, leaving an extra-long tail at the beginning. When I get to the final side, I trim the pieces as needed before machine stitching. Using a 2"-wide strip for binding also helps reduce bulk when binding coasters and other small items.*

## FINISHING THE COASTER

**1.** Layer the coaster top with batting and backing; baste the layers together.

**2.** Quilt by hand or machine. Sherri hand quilted in the ditch along the seamlines using a light-colored Aurifloss thread.

**3.** Use the navy 2"-wide strip to make double-fold binding and then attach the binding to the coaster.

CRYSTAL SKY TABLE MATES

# Amaryllis

*Watching my favorite Christmas movies as a child often had me wishing for a traditional Christmas scene with fluffy snowflakes covering the ground in a sea of white. Growing up in southern Nevada, though, we didn't see snow except on rare occasions. Even without the snow, I still find the holidays to be quite magical. I'm very fond of desert flowers that only bloom during the winter months. The poinsettia is one example, but another one of my favorites is the amaryllis flower. One species of amaryllis is native to South Africa and blooms there during the holidays. My brother-in-law lived in that area for two years, including a couple of holidays. This stunning flower is a beautiful shade of red and reminds me of his time spent there. ~ Chelsi*

**FINISHED QUILT: 60½" × 60½"**
**FINISHED BLOCK: 14" × 14"**

## MATERIALS

*Yardage is based on 42"-wide fabric. Fat quarters measure 18" × 21". Fabrics are Red Barn Christmas by Sweetwater for Moda Fabrics.*

* 2⅛ yards of white solid for block backgrounds and border
* 8 fat quarters of assorted red prints for blocks and binding
* 8 fat quarters of assorted green prints for blocks and binding
* 4 fat quarters of assorted gray prints for blocks
* 3¾ yards of fabric for backing
* 67" × 67" piece of batting

## CUTTING

*All measurements include ¼" seam allowances.*

**From the white solid, cut:**
5 strips, 3" × 42"; crosscut into 64 squares, 3" × 3"
21 strips, 2½" × 42"; crosscut *15 of the strips* into:
    64 pieces, 2½" × 6½"
    64 squares, 2½" × 2½"

**From *each* of the red prints, cut:**
12 squares, 3" × 3" (96 total)
8 squares, 2½" × 2½" (64 total)
2 strips, 2¼" × 9" (16 total)

**From *each* of the green prints, cut:**
12 squares, 3" × 3" (96 total)
8 squares, 2½" × 2½" (64 total)
2 strips, 2¼" × 9" (16 total)

**From *each* of the gray prints, cut:**
36 squares, 2½" × 2½" (144 total)

## MAKING THE BLOCKS

Press seam allowances in the directions indicated by the arrows.

**1.** Draw a diagonal line on the wrong side of the white 3" squares. Layer a marked square on a red or green 3" square, right sides together. Sew ¼" from both sides of the drawn line. Cut the unit apart on the marked line to make two half-square-triangle units. Trim the units to measure 2½" square. Make 64 green/white units and 64 red/white units.

Make 64 of each unit.

**2.** Using the remaining red and green 3" squares and marking on the wrong side of the lighter-colored squares, repeat step 1 to make 128 red/green half-square-triangle units. Trim the units to 2½" square.

Make 128 units.

## A Note from Sherri

*Chelsi's Amaryllis quilt is one of my favorites. She sent me a quick photo after she had her blocks laid out, and I could hardly wait to see it put together. I love the fabric combinations she picked and the half-blocks surrounding the center flowers.*

*Designed and pieced by Chelsi Stratton; quilted by Marion Bott*

**3.** Lay out two red/green units, two green/white units, one red 2½" square, one green 2½" square, one white 2½" square, and two gray 2½" squares in three rows as shown. The red and green prints should be the same throughout. Sew the units and squares into rows, and then join the rows. Make two matching units measuring 6½" square, including seam allowances. These will be your green units. Repeat to make two red units using two red/white units and swapping the placement of the red and green pieces as shown.

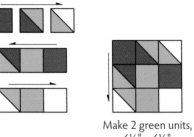

Make 2 green units,
6½" × 6½".

Make 2 red units,
6½" × 6½".

**4.** Repeat step 3 to make a total of 16 sets of four units each. You'll have two red and two green units in each set.

**5.** Lay out two red and two green units, four white 2½" × 6½" pieces, and one gray 2½" square in three rows. Sew the pieces into rows and then join the rows to make a block. Make 16 blocks measuring 14½" square, including seam allowances.

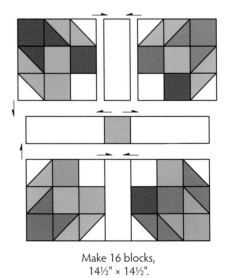

Make 16 blocks,
14½" × 14½".

## ASSEMBLING THE QUILT TOP

**1.** Referring to the quilt assembly diagram below and the photo on page 39, lay out the blocks in four rows of four blocks each, arranging them so that red units adjoin red units and green units adjoin green units. This will make red or green stars emerge once the blocks are joined.
Sew the blocks into rows and then join the rows. The quilt top should measure 56½" square, including seam allowances.

**2.** Join the remaining white 2½"-wide strips end to end. From the pieced strip, cut two 60½"-long strips and two 56½"-long strips. Sew the shorter strips to the left and right sides of the quilt center. Sew the longer strips to the top and bottom edges. The quilt top should measure 60½" square.

## FINISHING THE QUILT

**1.** Layer the quilt top with batting and backing; baste the layers together.

**2.** Quilt by hand or machine. The quilt shown is machine quilted with an allover Baptist fan design.

**3.** Use the red and green 2¼" × 9" strips to make scrappy double-fold binding and then attach the binding to the quilt.

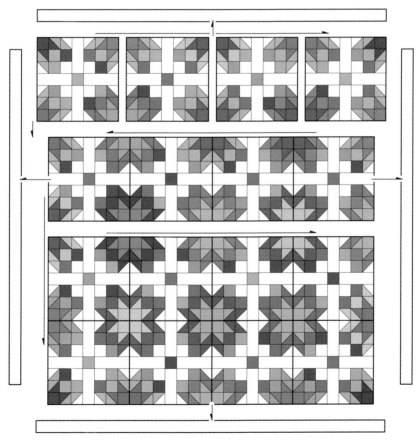

Quilt assembly

# Christmas Flowers Table Runner

*I love hexagons! So, of course, I had to include a project with Christmas hexagon flowers. I used three different red prints for the flowers, three different green prints for the flower centers, and light prints for the appliqué backgrounds. The green border and red gingham binding provided the perfect accents for this runner. ~ Sherri*

**FINISHED RUNNER: 17½" × 43½"**
**FINISHED BLOCK: 9" × 9"**

## MATERIALS

*Yardage is based on 42"-wide fabric. Fat quarters measure 18" × 21"; fat eighths measure 9" × 21".*

* 3 fat eighths of assorted red prints for flowers
* 3 pieces, 2½" × 3", of assorted green prints for flower centers
* 2 fat quarters of light prints for blocks*
* ⅛ yard of green dot for sashing
* ¼ yard of white solid for inner border
* ⅜ yard of green floral for outer border
* ⅓ yard of red gingham for binding
* 1½ yards of fabric for backing
* 24" × 50" piece of batting
* Cardstock or other sturdy paper for hexagon foundations OR 1" precut hexagon paper pieces
* Template plastic (optional)
* Paper punch (optional)

*You can also use 3 Layer Cake 10" squares: 2 from one light print and 1 from a different light print.*

## CUTTING

*All measurements include ¼" seam allowances.*

**From *each* of the red prints, cut:**
6 pieces, 2" × 3½" (18 total)

**From the light prints, cut a *total* of:**
3 squares, 9½" × 9½"

**From the green dot, cut:**
4 strips, 2½" × 9½"

**From the white solid, cut:**
3 strips, 1½" × 42"; crosscut into:
    2 strips, 1½" × 35½"
    2 strips, 1½" × 11½"

**From the green floral, cut:**
3 strips, 3½" × 42"; crosscut into:
    2 strips, 3½" × 37½"
    2 strips, 3½" × 17½"

**From the red gingham, cut:**
4 strips, 2¼" × 42"

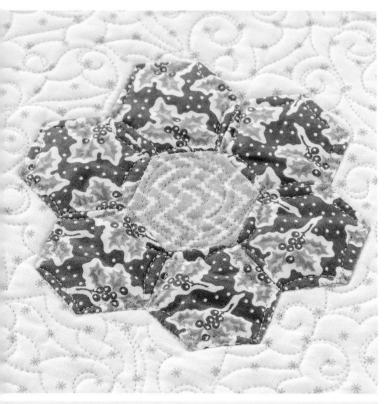

## MAKING THE BLOCKS

Skip steps 1 and 2 below if you have purchased precut foundation papers for 1" hexagons.

**1.** Trace the pattern on page 47 onto cardstock or template plastic. Cut it out just inside the traced lines to make a master template.

**2.** Trace the master template onto cardstock or sturdy paper 21 times. Cut out the paper hexagons just inside the traced lines. Be as accurate as possible when tracing and cutting so that all the shapes are exactly the same. Use a small paper punch (or scissors) to punch a hole in the center of each paper foundation.

**3.** Center a paper hexagon template on the wrong side of a red or green 2½" × 3" piece. Pin through the center of the hole without piercing the template. Use the template as a guide to cut out a fabric hexagon about ⅜" larger than the template on all sides. Prepare 18 red and 3 green hexagons (21 total).

Make 21 hexagons.

### Make It Easier

*Cutting a seam allowance that is ⅜" wide, instead of ¼" wide, on all sides of the hexagon template makes the basting process easier. You don't need an exact seam allowance, because the paper foundation will provide a precise shape. Punching a hole in the center of each template allows for much easier removal of the paper than if you baste or glue the template in place.*

**4.** Fold the seam allowance over the template. Using regular sewing thread, stitch through the folded corners of the fabric to hold it securely in place around the paper. Don't stitch through the template. After the entire hexagon is basted, knot and clip the thread. Make 18 red and 3 green hexagons (21 total).

Make 21 hexagons.

**5.** Place one green and one red hexagon right sides together, aligning the edges. With a single strand of thread, whipstitch them together from corner to corner, catching only the folded fabric edges. Repeat to join a total of six matching red hexagons to make a flower unit, attaching each red hexagon to the green hexagon first and then whipstitching the sides of the red hexagons together. Do not remove the papers. Make three flower units.

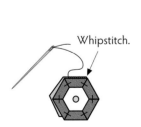

Whipstitch.

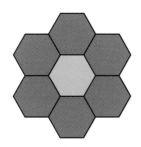

Make 3 flower units.

**6.** Pin a flower unit in the center of a light 9½" square. Appliqué in place using a small whipstitch. Carefully cut a small slit in the back of the block, underneath the flower unit. Remove the papers by inserting a toothpick in the punched hole. Press the block. Make three Grandmother's Flower Garden blocks measuring 9½" square, including seam allowances.

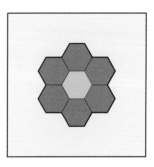

Make 3 blocks,
9½" × 9½".

## Perfectly Centered

*Fold a light square into quarters and lightly finger-press to establish centering lines for the hexagon flowers. After stitching, press the blocks and the lines will disappear. For pinning the flower units in place, small Clover appliqué pins are my favorites.*

*Designed and pieced by Sherri McConnell; quilted by Val Krueger*

## ASSEMBLING THE TABLE-RUNNER TOP

Press seam allowances in the directions indicated by the arrows.

**1.** Join the blocks and green dot strips, alternating their positions as shown in the table-runner assembly diagram below. The table runner should measure 9½" × 35½", including seam allowances.

**2.** Sew the white 1½" × 35½" strips to the long edges of the table runner. Sew the white 1½" × 11½" strips to the short ends of the runner. The table runner should measure 11½" × 37½", including seam allowances.

**3.** Sew the green floral 3½" × 37½" strips to the long edges of the table runner. Sew the green floral 3½" × 17½" strips to the short ends of the runner. The table runner should measure 17½" × 43½".

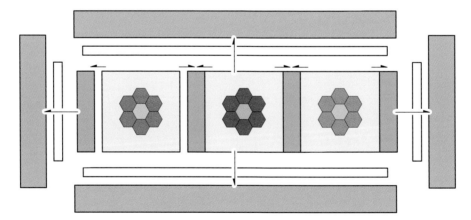

Table-runner assembly

## FINISHING THE TABLE RUNNER

**1.** Layer the table-runner top with batting and backing; baste the layers together.

**2.** Quilt by hand or machine. The table runner shown is machine quilted with outline stitching and loops in the hexagons, while the block background and inner border are stitched with loops and swirls. Diamond shapes are stitched in the green sashing and a diamond grid is stitched in the outer border.

**3.** Use the red gingham 2¼"-wide strips to make double-fold binding and then attach the binding to the table runner.

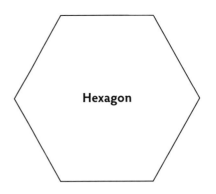

Hexagon

# Raspberry Jell-O Salad

*Each year I make this Raspberry Jell-O Salad. To me it's more like a dessert, but again, this is one dish the kids (who are all now adults) ask for each Christmas.*

2+ cups crushed pretzels*
¾ cup melted butter
1 large package (6 ounces) or
   2 small packages (3 ounces)
   raspberry JELL-O
2 cups boiling water
2½ cups frozen raspberries
8 ounces cream cheese, softened
1 cup plus 2 tablespoons sugar
8 ounces heavy whipping cream,
   whipped

*A rolling pin works well for crushing pretzels into small pieces.*

Preheat oven to 350°. Mix the crushed pretzels with the melted butter and two tablespoons of sugar and spread in the bottom of a 9" × 13" cake pan. Bake about 10 minutes, then remove from the oven and let cool. Dissolve the Jell-O in the boiling water and pour it into a 9" × 13" glass dish. Refrigerate until it starts to gel, then fold in the frozen raspberries and continue to refrigerate until set. Beat the cream cheese, one cup of sugar, and whipped cream together to make the dessert topping. Spread the topping over the Jell-O mixture and refrigerate until ready to serve. Just before serving, sprinkle the baked pretzels over the top of the dish.

# Mistletoe

*Who doesn't love a little mistletoe, or any excuse to show a loved one how much you care? Every Christmas season, my in-laws hang a small branch of mistletoe above the doorway of their home where they're sure to pass it on their way out. I have always found this to be a sweet tradition, since they never want to miss a chance to share their adoration for each other when they leave the house for the day. ~ Chelsi*

**FINISHED QUILT: 49½" × 65"**
**FINISHED BLOCK: 14" × 14"**

## MATERIALS

*Yardage is based on 42"-wide fabric. Fat quarters measure 18" × 21". Fabrics are Merry and Bright by Me & My Sister for Moda Fabrics.*

* 2⅝ yards of white solid for blocks, sashing, and border
* 6 fat quarters of assorted red prints for blocks and binding
* 6 fat quarters of assorted green prints for blocks
* ⅛ yard of green diagonal stripe for cornerstones
* 3⅛ yards of fabric for backing
* 56" × 71" piece of batting

## CUTTING

*All measurements include ¼" seam allowances.*

**From the white solid, cut:**
8 strips, 3" × 42"; crosscut into 96 squares, 3" × 3"
17 strips, 2½" × 42"; crosscut *11 of the strips* into:
    48 strips, 2½" × 6½"
    48 squares, 2½" × 2½"
9 strips, 2" × 42"; crosscut into 17 strips, 2" × 14½"

**From *each* of the assorted red prints, cut:**
4 squares, 4½" × 4½" (24 total)
8 squares, 3" × 3" (48 total)
1 square, 2½" × 2½" (6 total)
2 strips, 2¼" × 21" (12 total)

**From *each* of the assorted green prints, cut:**
4 squares, 4½" × 4½" (24 total)
8 squares, 3" × 3" (48 total)
1 square, 2½" × 2½" (6 total)

**From the green diagonal stripe, cut:**
6 squares, 2" × 2"

### Be Organized

*After cutting your fabrics, it's helpful to keep them separated by color and print. Visually, this particular quilt looks so pretty if you keep like colors and prints together. Plus, using an opposite color for the center square gives the quilt just enough contrast!*

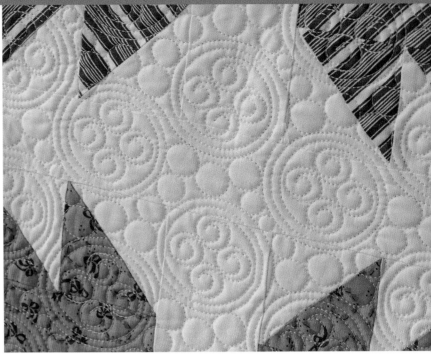

## MAKING THE BLOCKS

Press seam allowances in the directions indicated by the arrows.

**1.** Draw a diagonal line from corner to corner on the wrong side of the white 3" squares. Layer a marked square on a red or green print 3" square, right sides together. Sew ¼" from both sides of the drawn line. Cut the unit apart on the marked line to make two half-square-triangle units. Trim the units to measure 2½" square, including seam allowances. Make a total of 96 red and 96 green units.

2½"

2½"

2½"

2½"

Make 96 of each unit.

**2.** Lay out one white 2½" square, four matching red half-square-triangle units, and one matching red 4½" square as shown. Join the white square and two triangle units to make the top row. Join the remaining two triangle units and then sew the red square to the right edge to make the bottom row. Join the rows to make a corner unit measuring 6½" square, including seam allowances. Make six sets of four matching units.

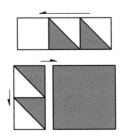 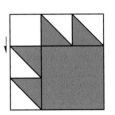

Make 6 sets of 4 matching units, 6½" × 6½".

**3.** Lay out four matching corner units, four white 2½" × 6½" strips, and one green print 2½" square in three rows as shown. Sew the pieces into rows and then join the rows to make a Mistletoe block. Make six red blocks measuring 14½" square, including seam allowances.

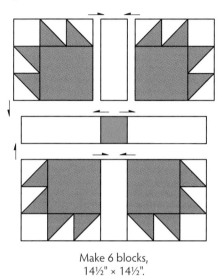

Make 6 blocks,
14½" × 14½".

**4.** Lay out one white 2½" square, four matching green half-square-triangle units, and one matching green print 4½" square as shown. Join the white square and two triangle units to make the top row. Join the remaining two triangle units and then sew the green square to the right edge to make the bottom row. Join the rows to make a corner unit measuring 6½" square, including seam allowances. Make six sets of four matching units.

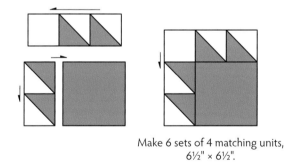

Make 6 sets of 4 matching units,
6½" × 6½".

**5.** Lay out four matching corner units, four white 2½" × 6½" strips, and one red 2½" square in three rows as shown. Sew the pieces into rows and

then join the rows to make a Mistletoe block. Make six green blocks measuring 14½" square, including seam allowances.

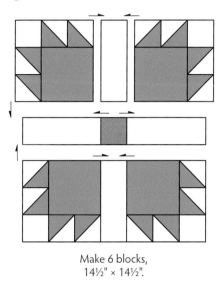

Make 6 blocks,
14½" × 14½".

## ASSEMBLING THE QUILT TOP

Refer to the quilt assembly diagram on page 53 as needed throughout.

**1.** Join two red blocks, one green block, and two white 2" × 14½" strips, alternating the red and green blocks to make a block row. Make two rows. Join two green blocks, one red block, and two white 2" × 14½" strips to make a block row. Make two rows. The rows should measure 14½" × 45½", including seam allowances.

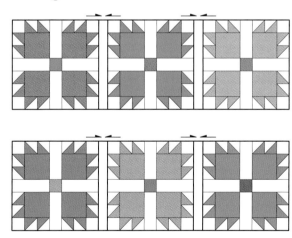

Make 2 of each row,
14½" × 45½".

*Pieced and designed by Chelsi Stratton; quilted by Marion Bott*

**2.** Join three white 2" × 14½" strips and two green stripe squares to make a sashing row. Make three rows measuring 2" × 45½", including seam allowances.

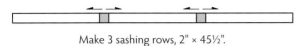

Make 3 sashing rows, 2" × 45½".

**3.** Join the block rows and sashing rows. The quilt top should measure 45½" × 61", including seam allowances.

**4.** Join the remaining white 2½"-wide strips end to end. From the pieced strip, cut two 61"-long strips and two 49½"-long strips. Sew the longer strips to the left and right sides of the quilt top. Sew the shorter strips to the top and bottom edges. The quilt top should measure 49½" × 65".

## FINISHING THE QUILT

**1.** Layer the quilt top with batting and backing; baste the layers together.

**2.** Quilt by hand or machine. The quilt shown is machine quilted with an allover circle and flower design.

**3.** Use the red 2¼"-wide strips to make scrappy double-fold binding and then attach the binding to the quilt.

Quilt assembly

MISTLETOE

# Farmhouse Flannel Quilt

*Everyone needs a cozy flannel quilt for the winter. This one is large enough to use on a bed but not so big that it can't also be draped over a sofa for snuggling under during chilly winter days and nights. The simplicity of the design allows the farmhouse flannels to shine. ~ Sherri*

**FINISHED QUILT: 64½" × 80½"**
**FINISHED BLOCK: 16" × 16"**

## MATERIALS

*Yardage is based on 42"-wide fabric. Fat quarters measure 18" × 21". Fabrics are Farmhouse Flannels by Lisa Bongean of Primitive Gatherings for Moda Fabrics.*

* ½ yard *each* of 9 assorted medium and dark flannels (referred to collectively as "dark") for blocks
* 8 fat quarters of assorted medium and dark flannels (referred to collectively as "dark") for blocks
* 2 fat quarters of light flannels for blocks
* ⅝ yard of gray flannel for binding
* 5 yards of fabric for backing
* 73" × 89" piece of batting

### Keep It Simple

Chelsi and I split a bundle of Farmhouse Flannels fat quarters. We both chose simple designs for our projects—Chelsi made the Scrappy Stripes Flannel Pillow (page 61) and I made this simple patchwork quilt. Since flannel is bulky, simple designs are easiest to prevent bulky seam intersections. You might also want to consider using a walking foot when sewing with flannel to keep the fabrics pulling evenly as you sew. ~ Sherri

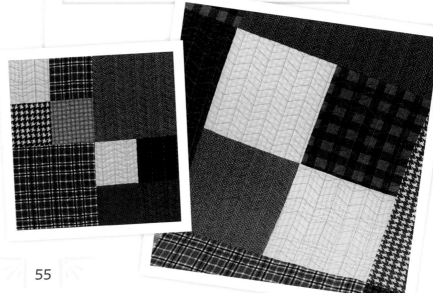

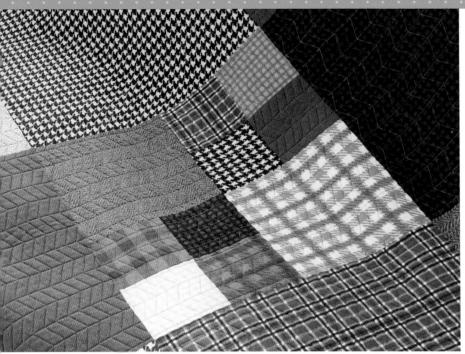

## A Note from Chelsi

*Growing up, we always had flannel quilts in our home. They were perfect for those cold winter months while we watched Christmas movies together as a family. This Farmhouse Flannel Quilt brings back those memories and will probably be one of the first projects I make from my mom's designs in this book.*

## CUTTING

*All measurements include ¼" seam allowances.*

**From *each* of the 9 dark ½-yard pieces, cut:**
1 square, 16½" × 16½" (9 total)
3 squares, 4½" × 4½" (27 total)

**From *each* of the 8 dark fat quarters, cut:**
4 squares, 8½" × 8½" (32 total)

**From *each* of the light fat quarters, cut:**
2 squares, 8½" × 8½" (4 total)
3 squares, 4½" × 4½" (6 total; 1 is extra)

**From the gray flannel, cut:**
8 strips, 2¼" × 42"

## MAKING THE BLOCKS

Press seam allowances in the directions indicated by the arrows.

**1.** Lay out four different light or dark 4½" squares in two rows. Sew the squares into rows, and then join the rows to make a four-patch unit. Make eight units measuring 8½" square, including seam allowances.

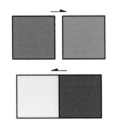

Make 8 units,
8½" × 8½".

*Designed and pieced by Sherri McConnell; quilted by Marion Bott*

## ASSEMBLING THE QUILT TOP

**1.** Lay out the dark 16½" squares, Four Patch blocks, and Double Four Patch blocks in five rows as shown in the quilt assembly diagram. Rearrange or rotate the blocks as needed for an even distribution of color and fabric. Sew the blocks and squares into rows, and then join the rows. The quilt top should measure 64½" × 80½".

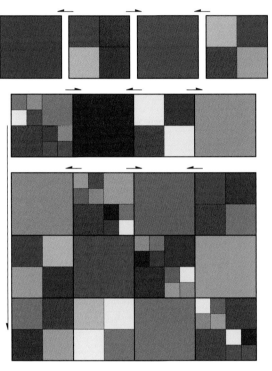

Quilt assembly

**2.** Lay out two four-patch units and two dark or light 8½" squares in two rows. Sew the units and squares into rows. Join the rows to make a Double Four Patch block. Make four blocks measuring 16½" square, including seam allowances.

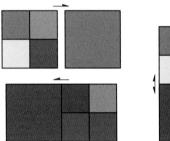
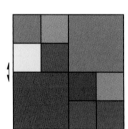

Make 4 Double Four Patch blocks, 16½" × 16½".

**3.** Lay out four different 8½" squares in two rows. Sew the squares into rows, and then join the rows to make a Four Patch block. Make seven blocks measuring 16½" square, including seam allowances.

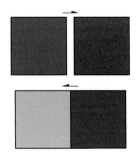

Make 7 Four Patch blocks 16½" × 16½".

**2.** Stitch around the perimeter of the quilt top, ⅛" from the outer edges, to lock the seams in place.

## FINISHING THE QUILT

**1.** Layer the quilt top with batting and backing; baste the layers together.

**2.** Quilt by hand or machine. The quilt shown is machine quilted with an allover herringbone design.

**3.** Use the gray 2¼"-wide strips to make double-fold binding and then attach the binding to the quilt.

# Christmas Morning Casserole

*I put this breakfast casserole together the night before Christmas so that we can pop it in the oven first thing on Christmas morning. While I often add another dish or two, this is the one that my children remember from their childhoods and that must be made each year.*

1 pound ham, cubed
8 ounces cheddar cheese, cubed
6 slices white bread with crusts cut off, cubed (you won't use the crusts)
3 eggs, beaten
2 cups milk
½ teaspoon dry mustard
2–4 tablespoons melted butter

Place the cubed ham, cheese, and bread into a 9" × 13" glass dish. Stir the eggs, milk, and dry mustard together in a small bowl and then pour over the ham, cheese, and bread mixture. Pour the melted butter over the top and cover with tin foil. Refrigerate overnight. The next morning, preheat oven to 325°. Bake 1 hour. Let sit 10 minutes before cutting into squares.

# Scrappy Stripes Flannel Pillow

*I absolutely love a rectangle pillow, especially if that pillow is made of soft, cozy flannel fabrics. It's the ideal simple piece of decor for just about any space in your home. This pillow project goes together quickly and adds the perfect touch of warmth wherever you need it. Place it on the center of a couch, bed, or even a hallway bench! ~ Chelsi*

**FINISHED PILLOW: 30½" × 15½"**

## MATERIALS

*Yardage is based on 42"-wide fabric. Fabrics are Farmhouse Flannels by Lisa Bongean of Primitive Gatherings for Moda Fabrics.*

* 15 strips, 2½" × 15½", of assorted light and dark flannels for patchwork
* ⅜ yard of light gray flannel for zipper flap and binding
* ⅝ yard of dark gray flannel for pillow back
* 22" × 37" piece of muslin for quilt-sandwich backing
* 22" × 37" piece of batting
* 15" × 30" pillow form
* 32" zipper

## CUTTING

*All measurements include ¼" seam allowances.*

**From the light gray flannel, cut:**
1 strip, 4" × 30½"
3 strips, 2¼" × 42"

**From the dark gray flannel, cut:**
2 strips, 8" × 30½"

### Be Creative

*Give this project a fun look by mixing up the assortment of strips. This pillow works perfectly without a uniform layout of prints and colors.*

*Pieced and designed by Chelsi Stratton; quilted by Gail Begay*

### A Note from Sherri

*Chelsi's scrappy pillow is the perfect companion to my Farmhouse Flannel Quilt (page 55). We both chose simple blocks when working with the flannels, and I love how the designs in these two projects complement each other.*

## ASSEMBLING THE PILLOW TOP

**1.** Join the flannel 2½" × 15½" strips side by side to make a pillow top measuring 30½" × 15½", including seam allowances. Press the seam allowances open.

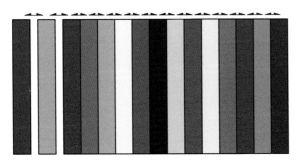

Make 1 pillow top,
30½" × 15½".

**2.** Layer the pillow top, batting, and muslin piece; baste the layers together. Quilt by hand or machine. The pillow top shown is machine quilted with a straight line in the center of each strip.

**3.** Trim the excess batting and backing even with the pillow top.

## MAKING THE PILLOW BACK

Refer to "Making the Pillow Back" on page 27 of the Christmas Star Pillow project for detailed illustrations.

**1.** Press the light gray 4" × 30½" strip in half, wrong sides together, so that it measures 2" × 30½". This will be the zipper flap.

**2.** Align the flap right sides together with the raw edge of a dark gray strip. Place the zipper along the raw edges, right sides together. The zipper edge should be aligned with the raw edges of the flap and pillow back. Any extra zipper length should extend beyond the fabric. It will be trimmed later. Use a zipper foot to sew the zipper using a ¼" seam allowance.

**3.** Place the second dark gray strip right sides together with the unsewn side of the zipper, aligning the zipper edge with the raw edge of the pillow back. Pin and sew the zipper in place using a ¼" seam allowance and a zipper foot.

**4.** Press the seam with the flap so that it covers the zipper; topstitch ¼" from the flap seam.

## FINISHING THE PILLOW

**1.** Place the pillow front on the pillow back, wrong sides together. Unzip the zipper partway so that the zipper pull is in the center of the pillow. Pin and sew around the edges using a ¼" seam allowance. Trim any excess length from the end of the zipper.

**2.** Use the light gray 2¼"-wide strips to make double-fold binding and then bind the pillow as you would a quilt.

**3.** Unzip the pillow. Insert the pillow form and close the zipper.

# Old-Fashioned Apple Crisp

I cannot think about the Christmas season without pairing it with some of my favorite recipes. My mom always made a few specific dishes during the holidays that my siblings and I looked forward to every year. One of my favorites was a treat that she baked occasionally, her Old-Fashioned Apple Crisp. It's warm, tangy, sweet, and even better served with vanilla ice cream!

4 cups sliced,
    peeled tart
    apples
    (about 3 medium)
¾ cup packed brown sugar
½ cup all-purpose flour
½ cup rolled oats
1 teaspoon ground cinnamon
¼ teaspoon allspice
⅓ cup cold butter
Vanilla ice cream (optional)

Preheat oven to 375°. Place apples in greased 8" square baking dish. Combine brown sugar, flour, oats, cinnamon, and allspice; cut in butter until crumbly. Sprinkle over apples. Bake 30–35 minutes or until apples are tender. Serve warm with ice cream if desired.

# Ornamental Table Topper

*I'm always looking for ways to make sure every space in my home has some festive and cozy decorations during the Christmas season! A table topper is the perfect way to show off some of your favorite Christmas fabrics and spruce up the dining table. ~ Chelsi*

**FINISHED TOPPER: 27½" × 27½"**
**FINISHED BLOCK: 6" × 6"**

## MATERIALS

*Yardage is based on 42"-wide fabric. Fat eighths measure 9" × 21". Fabrics are Christmas Morning by Vanessa Goertzen of Lella Boutique for Moda Fabrics.*

* 8 fat eighths of assorted red prints for blocks and binding
* 8 fat eighths of assorted green prints for blocks
* 8 fat eighths of assorted gray prints for blocks
* ¼ yard of white solid for border
* 1 yard of fabric for backing
* 32" × 32" piece of batting

## CUTTING

*All measurements include ¼" seam allowances.*

**From *each* of the assorted red prints, cut:**
2 pieces, 2½" × 6½" (16 total)
1 strip, 2¼" × 16" (8 total)

**From *each* of the assorted green prints, cut:**
2 pieces, 2½" × 6½" (16 total)

**From *each* of the assorted gray prints, cut:**
2 pieces, 2½" × 6½" (16 total)

**From the white solid, cut:**
4 strips, 2" × 42"; crosscut into:
    2 strips, 2" × 27½"
    2 strips, 2" × 24½"

### Time-Saver

*All of the blocks in this table topper use the exact same color scheme, so after you have laid out your blocks, simply put them all into one pile and chain piece them. This will save you so much time, and you'll find that this project goes together quickly!*

## MAKING THE BLOCKS

Press seam allowances in the directions indicated by the arrows.

Lay out one red, one gray, and one green 2½" × 6½" piece as shown. Join the pieces to make a block. Make 16 blocks measuring 6½" square, including seam allowances.

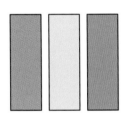

Make 16 blocks,
6½" × 6½".

## ASSEMBLING THE TABLE TOPPER

**1.** Referring to the table-topper assembly diagram at right, lay out the blocks in four rows of four blocks each, rotating every other block as shown. Sew the blocks into rows and then join the rows. The table topper should measure 24½" square, including seam allowances.

**2.** Sew the white 2" × 24½" strips to the left and right sides of the topper. Sew the white

2" × 27½" strips to the top and bottom edges. The table topper should measure 27½" square.

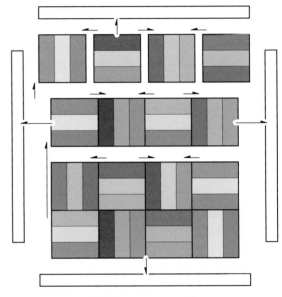

Table-topper assembly

## FINISHING THE TABLE TOPPER

**1.** Layer the table-topper top with batting and backing; baste the layers together.

**2.** Quilt by hand or machine. The table topper shown is machine quilted with an allover design of leaves and circles.

**3.** Use the red 2¼"-wide strips to make scrappy double-fold binding and then attach the binding to the table topper.

Chelsi's Ornamental Table Topper is a fast and fun Rail Fence block variation. After seeing this one, I had to let Chelsi know that my grandmother used the Rail Fence block just about as frequently as any other block design. She loved featuring it in pillows and place mats, so I was super happy to see that Chelsi had made a darling table topper with the design.

**Designed and pieced by Chelsi Stratton; quilted by Gail Begay**

ORNAMENTAL TABLE TOPPER

# Classic Tree Skirt

*Other than a quilted patchwork pillow I made as a teenager; my first "quilt" was actually a patchwork tree skirt I made for our first family Christmas. I remember going to the fabric store to pick out a variety of fabrics. I cut squares using scissors and a cardboard template. And then I tied the intersecting squares with yarn and added lace to the outer edges. That tree skirt served us well for many years. And while I've made several fun quilted tree skirts since, I've always wanted to re-create that first tree skirt (minus the cardboard templates, of course!). This one is perfectly sized for charm squares (or use a Layer Cake)—no templates required. ~ Sherri*

**FINISHED TREE SKIRT: 50" diameter**

## MATERIALS

*Yardage is based on 42"-wide fabric. Fabrics are Red Barn Christmas by Sweetwater for Moda Fabrics.*

* 121 squares, 5" × 5", of assorted red, green, and light prints for patchwork
* ¾ yard of green print for binding and ties
* 3¼ yards of fabric for backing
* 58" × 58" piece of batting
* 5" × 5" square of freezer paper
* 4½" circle template or small plate
* String

## CUTTING

*All measurements include ¼" seam allowances.*

**From the green print, cut on the *bias*:**
2¼"-wide strips to total 240"

### Organization Tip

*I alternated prints that were mostly red, mostly green, and mostly light so that those prints were in diagonal lines in the layout. This resulted in a fun, scrappy mix of prints without too much thinking on my part.*
*~ Sherri*

*A Note from Chelsi*

*I'm so glad that Mom decided to include a fun tree skirt. This classic version reminds me of the homemade skirt she stitched for our family Christmas trees while I was growing up. I love the simple patchwork in this one, which displays all of the fabrics so beautifully.*

## ASSEMBLING THE TREE SKIRT

Press seam allowances in the directions indicated by the arrows.

**1.** Lay out the assorted print squares in 11 rows of 11 squares each as shown in the tree-skirt assembly diagram, arranging the squares to form a diagonal lines of color. Sew the squares into rows and then join the rows. The tree-skirt top should measure 50" square, including seam allowances.

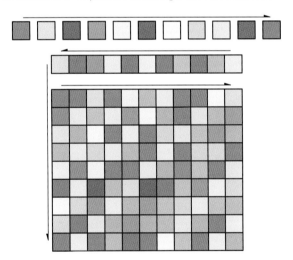

Tree-skirt assembly

**2.** Layer the tree-skirt top with batting and backing; baste the layers together.

**3.** Quilt by hand or machine. The tree skirt shown is machine quilted with an allover pattern of interlocking diamond shapes.

**4.** Tie the ends of a length of string to two pencils so that the pencils are 25" apart. Place the tip of one pencil in the center of the quilted tree skirt. Keeping the string fully extended, draw a circle for the outer edge of the tree skirt. Cut directly on the marked line.

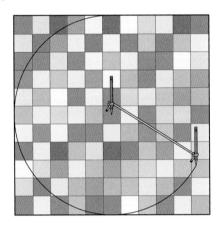

**5.** Choose which portion of the tree skirt will be the back. Using a rotary cutter and a long ruler, cut the tree skirt from the outer edge to the center square, cutting through the center of a row of squares.

Cut.

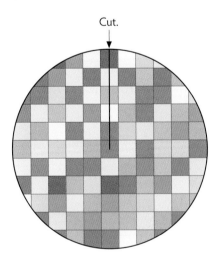

**6.** Use a small plate or a circle template to draw a 4½"-diameter circle on the dull side of the freezer paper. Cut out the circle on the marked line. Press the freezer-paper circle onto the center square. Cut around the freezer paper to make the center circle.

### Creative Coasters

*The tree skirt can easily be sized up or down as needed. Make an adorable mini tree skirt using 2½" squares. Here's a bonus for you. I couldn't bear to throw away all of the quilted pieces left over after I trimmed my patchwork into a circle. So, I used a Creative Grids round ruler to cut circles to use for coasters. I made large coasters that are 6½" diameter and a small coaster from the 4½"-diameter circle cut from the center of the tree skirt. ~ Sherri*

## FINISHING THE TREE SKIRT

**1.** Use the green 2¼"-wide bias strips to make double-fold binding. To attach the binding, start at the end on one side of the center circle. Sew along the straight edge, around the outer edges, and up the other straight edge. Trim the end of the binding.

**2.** Attach binding to the center circle, leaving a 12" tail on each side for the ties. You can trim the tails to the desired length after stitching, but it's nice to have plenty of length initially. Fold the binding tails in half (so they're the same width as the finished binding on the tree skirt) and machine stitch along the open edge of each tie.

*Designed and pieced by Sherri McConnell; quilted by Marion Bott*

# Poinsettia

*Every year during the Christmas season, Mom would buy poinsettias to display in our home. I looked forward to the beautiful seasonal flowers every year and it became a tradition she may not even realize she had started! This project is near and dear to my heart with the sweet poinsettia Flower blocks and accent of nine patches. Poinsettias symbolize good cheer and success and are said to bring wishes of celebration. ~ Chelsi*

**FINISHED QUILT: 64½" × 64½"**
**FINISHED BLOCK: 12" × 12"**

## MATERIALS

*Yardage is based on 42"-wide fabric. Fat quarters measure 18" × 21". Fabrics are Hustle and Bustle by Basic Grey for Moda Fabrics.*

* 3 yards of white solid for blocks and border
* 9 fat quarters of assorted red prints for blocks and binding
* 4 fat quarters of assorted green print for blocks
* 4 yards of fabric for backing
* 71" × 71" piece of batting

### ⊰ *Fabric Choices* ⊱

*This quilt is fun to make and even more fun to make scrappy! Don't be afraid to mix various prints of each coordinating color. This gives the quilt a fun look and the different prints create movement and interest.* ✳

## CUTTING

*All measurements include ¼" seam allowances.*

**From the white solid, cut:**
4 strips, 6½" × 42"; crosscut into 24 squares, 6½" × 6½"
28 strips, 2½" × 42"; crosscut *21 of the strips* into:
    13 strips, 2½" × 12½"
    26 strips, 2½" × 6½"
    174 squares, 2½" × 2½"

**From *each* of the assorted red prints, cut:**
5 strips, 2½" × 21"; crosscut into:
    3 strips, 2½" × 10½" (27 total; 1 is extra)
    3 strips, 2½" × 8½" (27 total; 1 is extra)
    14 squares, 2½" × 2½" (126 total; 6 are extra)
2 strips, 2¼" × 21" (18 total)

**From *each* of the assorted green prints, cut:**
5 strips, 2½" × 21"; crosscut into:
    7 pieces, 2½" × 4½" (28 total; 2 are extra)
    20 squares, 2½" × 2½" (80 total; 2 are extra)

## MAKING THE DOUBLE NINE PATCH BLOCKS

Press seam allowances in the directions indicated by the arrows.

**1.** Lay out five different red and four white 2½" squares in three rows. Sew the squares into rows and then join the rows to make a nine-patch unit. Make 24 units measuring 6½" square, including seam allowances.

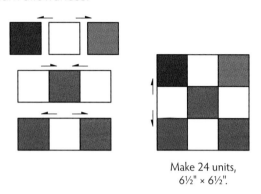

Make 24 units,
6½" × 6½".

**2.** Lay out two nine-patch units and two white 6½" squares in two rows. Sew the pieces into rows and then join the rows to make a Double Nine Patch block. Make 12 blocks measuring 12½" square, including seam allowances.

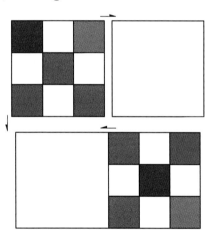

Make 12 Double Nine Patch blocks,
12½" × 12½".

## MAKING THE FLOWER BLOCKS

**1.** Draw a diagonal line from corner to corner on the wrong side of the remaining white 2½" squares and 52 green 2½" squares.

**2.** Place a marked white square on one end of a red 2½" × 10½" strip, noting the direction of the marked line. Sew on the marked line. Trim the excess corner fabric ¼" from the stitched line. Place a marked green square on the opposite end of the strip, again noting the direction of the marked line. Make 13 A units measuring 2½" × 10½", including seam allowances. Repeat to make 13 reversed A units, making sure to reverse the orientation of the marked lines.

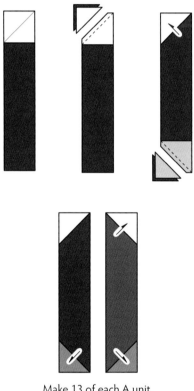

Make 13 of each A unit,
2½" × 10½".

**3.** Place a marked white square on one end of a red 2½" × 8½" strip, noting the direction of the marked line. Sew on the marked line. Trim the excess corner fabric ¼" from the stitched line. Place a marked green square on the opposite end of the strip, again noting the direction of the marked line. Make 13 B units measuring 2½" × 8½", including seam allowances. Repeat to make 13 reversed B units, making sure to reverse the orientation of the marked lines.

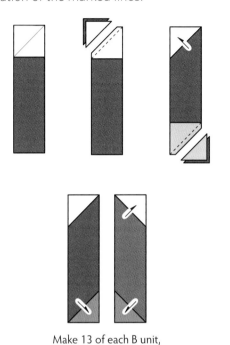

Make 13 of each B unit,
2½" × 8½".

**4.** Place a marked white square on one end of a green 2½" × 4½" piece, noting the direction of the marked line. Sew on the marked line. Trim the excess corner fabric ¼" from the stitched line. Make 13 C units measuring 2½" × 4½", including seam allowances. Repeat to make 13 reversed C units, making sure to reverse the orientation of the marked lines.

Make 13 of each C unit,
2½" × 4½".

POINSETTIA

## A Note from Sherri

I am so happy that Chelsi designed this lovely Poinsettia quilt for our book. Of course, I love poinsettias at Christmas, as did my grandmother. Chelsi's design is fun and modern and would also make a delightful four-block wall hanging.

*Designed and pieced by Chelsi Stratton; quilted by Marion Bott*

**5.** Sew a green square to one end of a white 2½" × 6½" strip to make unit D. Make 26 units measuring 2½" × 8½", including seam allowances.

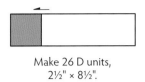

Make 26 D units,
2½" × 8½".

**6.** Lay out one unit each from steps 2–5 and one white 2½" × 12½" strip as shown. Sew an A unit to a reversed A unit. Sew a D unit to a B unit, and add a C unit to the bottom edge. Sew a D unit to a reversed B unit, and add a reversed C unit to the bottom edge. Join the three sections and then sew the white strip to the top edge. Repeat to make a total of 13 Flower blocks measuring 12½" square, including seam allowances.

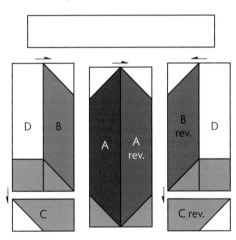

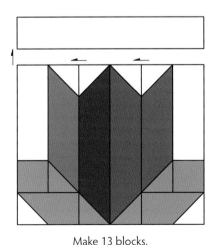

Make 13 blocks,
12½" × 12½".

## ASSEMBLING THE QUILT TOP

**1.** Referring to the quilt assembly diagram below, lay out the blocks in five rows of five blocks each, alternating the blocks in each row and from row to row. Sew the blocks into rows and then join the rows. The quilt top should measure 60½" square, including seam allowances.

**2.** Join the remaining white 2½"-wide strips end to end. From the pieced strip, cut two 64½"-long strips and two 60½"-long strips. Sew the shorter strips to the left and right sides of the quilt top. Sew the longer strips to the top and bottom edges. The quilt top should measure 64½" square.

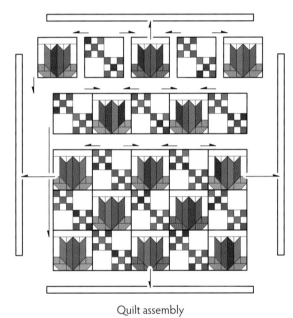

Quilt assembly

## FINISHING THE QUILT

**1.** Layer the quilt top with batting and backing; baste the layers together.

**2.** Quilt by hand or machine. The quilt shown is machine quilted with an allover teardrop and flower design.

**3.** Use the red 2¼"-wide strips to make scrappy double-fold binding and then attach the binding to the quilt.

# Sherri's Quilted Christmas Traditions

I like to make a new Christmas quilt each year. Often, I do Christmas sewing in the summer, but recently it's been a lot of fun to sew with Christmas fabrics in the fall. I also make some new place mats and Christmas pot holders just about every year. And I try to gift simple Christmas projects like runners, ornaments, and pot holders to friends and family every Christmas season. In this way, I feel like I'm in keeping with the spirit of what my grandmother did each year.

Something else I like to do each year is create handmade ornaments. This is also a tradition I've carried on from my grandmother. While she sometimes purchased ornaments from her travels, she also made ornaments for our family each year using a variety of techniques: plastic canvas, crochet, quilting, and even painting wooden ornaments.

## TRADITIONAL CHRISTMAS DECOR IDEAS

I love using quilts in my decor and have created a process over the years that makes decorating with my quilts and quilted items simple and fun.

First, I bring all of my Christmas quilted items out of their storage spaces and place everything in one landing space (usually the dining room table). I then begin to distribute the quilts first (excluding quilts that are used on beds). I like to drape quilts over the arms and backs of sofas, use them in stacks on top of cupboards, and occasionally roll them up to set in baskets. I also place table runners and toppers on all of the flat surfaces and roll up some smaller toppers and place them in an antique ceramic crock. Small pillows are arranged on shelves or put in bowls, while larger pillows are placed on sofas and chairs. Only after I've put out all of my quilts do I begin to set up the rest of my decorations. Sometimes I change things up from year to year, but with some items I like to keep a record of where they best fit or work, so I've listed many of the items along with their storage space and decor-use space in my copy of *A Quilting Life Monthly Planner*.

## CHRISTMAS PROJECT PLANNING

Christmas project planning is a yearlong effort for me. Often the best time to get ideas for Christmas projects you might want to make is during the holiday season itself. I'll make notes as I set out my decorations each year for something I think of while decorating. I also pay attention as I visit the homes of friends and family in order to get ideas of Christmas decor items to give. Finally, I also seem to think of ideas as I'm putting things away each year. I keep my Christmas projects and decor ideas in my *A Quilting Life Monthly Planner* so that I have the notes ready to refer to at any given time.

## CHRISTMAS FABRIC STORAGE

Since I like to work on Christmas projects throughout the year (and sometimes on a whim when I think of an idea), I keep my Christmas fabrics organized and easily accessible all year long. I don't mix my Christmas fabric scraps with other fabrics, keeping them instead in a couple of separate bins. Recently I've started a Jelly Roll strip bin of leftover Christmas fabrics along with a charm square bin. But I also keep many of my scraps of Christmas fabric together by collection when there is enough left over to make a complete project. I like being able to easily make a small project from the coordinated leftovers of a larger quilt or project without having to think too much about picking the fabrics. This makes it easier for me to make quick gifts without too much planning. Finally, I also have a Christmas orphan block bin where I keep leftover blocks from Christmas projects. These orphan blocks are often easy to turn into small pillows, mug rugs, or even table toppers.

# About the Authors

## SHERRI MCCONNELL

I was not going to be a quilter. My grandmother was a quilter, and she cut up perfectly good fabrics just to sew them back together. She hand quilted in the evenings with her stand-up frame and her lap frame. She made quilts, wall hangings, place mats, and table runners. And she gifted many lovely things to me and her other family members.

But because of her, and with her help, I made my very first quilt. Over the years, I found more and more time to sew. I also discovered the wide world of quilting blogs with inspiration at my fingertips. And I met the most wonderful and amazing people who love quilting as I do, as my grandmother did, and as her grandmothers did before her.

I am a quilter! I'm thankful for the encouragement and support of both my family members and the quilting community that I know online and in real life. Happy quilting!

## CHELSI STRATTON

I had decided pretty early on that I wasn't going to quilt. My mom had gently encouraged me for years. As I got older, I found the fabrics she was sewing with to be quite beautiful and my interest was suddenly piqued.

Later on, my mom brought up the idea of designing our own fabric. I knew immediately that was something I really wanted to do. We submitted our fabric designs to Moda Fabrics as a mother-daughter team and started officially designing for them soon afterward. It has been a dream come true and such a sweet thing to work alongside each other.

Designing fabric led to quilting, which is now my very favorite thing to do! I'm a quilter, a mom, a wife, a friend, and a designer. I'm blessed to have a supportive family and quilting community through it all and I'm so grateful for my quilting journey.